THE GREATEST 125 TIPS FOR TRIATHLON

ACCOMPLISH YOUR BEST TRIATHLON IRONMAN WITH THE BEST ADVICE

MARIANA CORREA

Copyright Page

2017 THE GREATEST 125
TIPS FOR TRIATHLON

ISBN 1979057745

Acknowledgement

To my father, words cannot express how grateful I am for everything you have done for me.

About the author

Mariana Correa is a certified professional coach and former professional tennis player. Mariana reached a career high of 26 in the world in juniors with wins over Anna Ivanovich (former #1 WTA in the world) and many other top 100 WTA players.
She competed successfully all over the world in over 26 countries and hundreds of cities including in London for Wimbledon, Paris for the French Open and in Australia for the world championships. She also represented Ecuador in Fed Cup, where the team reached the finals in their group.
During her career she was awarded the fair play award many times, proving to be not only an excellent player, but also a role model for other athletes.
Mariana is also a certified sports nutritionist with years of experience in proper nutrition and hydration for high performance athletes.
She combines her love and knowledge in sports in this book to provide you with all the information you need to succeed.
Description

THE BEST 125 TIPS FOR TRIATHLON will inspire you to become the best triathlete you can be.

With Brilliant advice that ranges from:

- Triathlon Training
- Triathlon Transitions
- Mental Training
- The Right Nutrition for you
- Hydrating Correctly
- Road Safety
- The Best Gear Advice
- Triathlon Race Preparation
- And so much more...

The secret is in the details, this book will tell you how to be the best triathlete you can be, by training and racing smarter.
Every aspect of your life has the potential to affect your mental and physical performance which is why this book addresses everything from rest, nutrition, hydration, recuperation, training, competing and much more.
Use these tips from start to finish so can feel confident and comfortable with your triathlon.
This book is the Perfect gift for any triathlon enthusiast including yourself.

Table of Contents

TIP #1

Get started today!
Your dreams are waiting for you, the
sooner you begin the closer you will
be to achieving them.

TIP #2

Work your weakness. It's easy to run
every day if that's your strongest, but
don't neglect your weaknesses. Keep
a training log so you can keep track of
what you need to work on.

TIP #3

Be SMART with your goals.

Be **SMART** with your goal setting.

Specific- Be clear about what you could like toattain.

Measureable - Establish your goals so you may see your progress in numbers.

Attainable - Make the goals realistic.

Relevant - It must make sense.

Time bound – Allow a time frame in which these goals must be achieved

TIP #4

Run more. By running more you'll improve your base fitness which will have your overall endurance.

TIP #5

Do what you love.
The only way to push yourself day in and day out is if you truly love what you do.

TIP #6

Have a Training plan.
This way you can stay organized with
your workouts and see your progress.

TIP #7

Surround yourself with knowledgeable
individuals. Listening and learning are
more valuable than thinking you
already know it all.

TIP #8

Be flexible with your training.
If it's a really hot day, you might want
to swim instead of run, or it's
swimming you can do some cross
training.

TIP #9

Being the best is great, but being the
best team is even better. Having
people around you who are great will
continue to challenge and motivate
you to strive for more.

TIP #10

Keep it fun.
You can work hard and still have a
great time while doing it.

TIP #11

Keep a Training Log.
Recording your activity is a great way
to motivate yourself as well by being
able to look back at all the goals that
have already achieved.

TIP #12

Hire a coach.
The proper technique with running,
swimming and cycling will help you
improve your time, endurance and
overall performance.

TIP #13

Train to be perfect.
Don't conform yourself with being
average. "Shoot for the moon, that
way you'll land within the stars."

TIP #14

Keep your training time compact.
There is no need to train all day,
instead focus on a good quality
workout.

TIP #15

Make sure you have the right
motivation surrounding you. It's a lot
easier to push yourself when you have
others around you encouraging you to
succeed.

TIP #16

Focus on your core.
By strengthening your core, you will avoid injuries by reinforcing underlying muscles such as hips, glutes and more.

TIP #17

Stay Positive!
Some days things might not go your way, don't let those days get you down, keep moving forward.

TIP #18

Have a training buddy.
It's always a good idea to have a
training partner to help each other and
stay competitive.

TIP #19

Be confident in yourself and your abilities. Understand confidence is not an emotion. I often hear the words, I feel confident or I don't feel confident today. Confidence is NOT an emotion.
Confidence is a belief, therefore it's a thought, and thoughts can be controlled.

TIP #20

Learn to tune your own bike.
Not only will you be saving a lot of
money, but you will get an even better
understanding of your bike.

TIP #21

Engage in positive Self Talk.
Who is your biggest fan? Well,
yourself of course. Pump yourself up!

$\mathcal{TIP}$ #22

Rent to Start.
When you are first trying out new
gear, it's best to rent or borrow to get
a good feel for the equipment before
fully investing in them.

TIP #23

Every action you do sends signals to your opponent and everyone around you. As much as a positive body language boosts an athlete's confidence, a negative body language gives indications to the opponent and makes the athlete helpless to attack and ultimately destruction.

TIP #24

Invest in a Good Triathlon Suit.
There is a lot of gear involved in
triathlon, but the most basic one would
be your Triathlon Suit, make sure you
feel comfortable in yours.

TIP #25

Fake it until you make it.
Champions are often talking to their
alter ego and pumping themselves up.
Even if it doesn't work at first, a
positive body language expresses to
the mind that the athlete is growing in
confidence which ultimately builds the
mental fortitude.

TIP #26

Always stay safe.
Remember to always wear your
helmet when you cycle, and never
swim in dangerous currents.

TIP #27

Be a creature of Habit.
Training is where habits and muscle
memory are created, good or bad.
This accentuates the importance
of *how we train*.

TIP #28

Try to at least once per month swim in open water. It's very different to swim in open water or indoors and most competitions take place outdoors.

TIP #29

ALWAYS Remember to Warm up before training or competing, no matter how late or rushed you are. Even if it's just 5 to 10 minutes, this is essential to prevent injuries which could keep you sidelined.

TIP #30

ALWAYS Remember to Stretch after training or competing, no matter how late or rushed you are. Stretching will allows your muscle to expand preventing soreness, and increasing their range of mobility.

TIP #31

Close your eyes.
When swim training close your eyes in a lap pool for 9-10 strokes, open your eyes and see towards which side you veer towards, begin correcting this until you swim straight.

TIP #32

Improve your Flexibility.
Take at least 1 hour per week to
improve your flexibility, you will
recover faster, prevent more injuries,
improve your posture and much more.

TIP #33

Don't overextend your joints when
stretching. Stretching is for the
muscles, not the joints or ligaments.
Hyperextending further than you can,
will actually lead to injuries.

TIP #34

Focus on your Key Workouts.
When working on your training plan
schedule your hardest workouts for
when you're fresh.

TIP #35

Practice Bricking.
In Triathlon, this would mean to do 2 of the sports back to back. You wouldn't need to do the full distances on both, it's mostly to practice for the muscle changeover. This is most common from cycling to running.

TIP #36

Pace yourself.
Don't start speeding only to finish slow, find a good rhythm and stick to it.

TIP #37

Visualize Success.
The best athletes in the world practice visualization, in order to achieve something you must first see it in your mind.

TIP #38

Learn to run tall.
When you run and exhaustion kicks in, your body might begin to hunch, fight this urge and keep your body aligned when running.

TIP #39

Rest to be the Best.
The strain from exercise is great but
not allowing your body to properly
recuperate will lead to injury, reduced
performance, and burnout.

TIP #40

Before an event get to know the
course. Scout the surroundings.

TIP #41

Begin Recuperation Immediately after finishing your training or competition. Ideally within 15-60 minutes after completing the last exercise refuel your body with a fruit, protein shake, energy bar, or sports drink.

TIP #42

There is no substitute for a good night rest. Sleep is equally as important as exercise and nutrition to any athlete who wishes to be successful.

TIP #43

Do a dry test triathlon.
If possible arrive ahead of time, and
get in the water, check out the
temperatures and the currents. Run
and cycle some of the course, check
for turns and elevations.

TIP #44

Practice organizing your Transition Area. Every second counts, the more coordinated your area is, the better.

TIP #45

Practice your transitions.
Go through the complete process, take off your wetsuit and get into your cycling gear, the into your running gear.

TIP #46

Have a Nutritional Plan.
According to your weight and your
energy expenditures, you need to
know exactly how much you need to
consume with each meal.

TIP #47

Test your gear.
While you are trying out the course,
make sure your gear is working well.

TIP #48

Do not buy new shoes or gear for the
race. You might get blisters, or not feel
completely comfortable with your new
gear.

TIP #49

Tune up your bike.
If your tires are old, make sure to
replace the tubes.

TIP #50

Label your gear.
Mark all your belongings (wetsuit,
helmet, running and biking shoes,
etc.) with a permanent marker.

TIP #51

Train your gut.
Nourish your body the same way you would during a competition to get used to it.

TIP #52

Keep your future champion body healthy by choosing a variety of foods and keeping your plate colorful. It is a balance of nutrients that keeps athletes healthy and at maximum performance.

TIP #53

SKIP THE EMPTY CALORIES.
While cake and soda might taste
good, they will hinder performance
and decrease overall good health.

TIP #54

Increase protein in your meals post training or competing. You will need protein to assist in repairing and rebuilding muscle that was broken down during exercise.

TIP #55

Increase your carbohydrates in your meals before training or competing. They are the most important source of energy while exercising, carbs provide the energy that fuels muscle contractions.

TIP #56

Keep your meals as colorful as possible with fruits and vegetables. A greater variety of vitamins and minerals will improve your health and performance.

TIP #57

Keep Healthy Snacks always with you. Fruits, Vegetables (fresh, dry or dehydrated) and Nuts are a great way to keep hunger at bay and your body properly nourished.

TIP #58

Get a race belt.
No need for pins, you can attach your number to the belt, flip it to your back for cycling and switch it forward for running.

TIP #59

Organize and compartmentalize.
You should have several bags for your gear. Separate according to running gear, swimming gear and bike gear.

$\mathcal{TIP}$ #60

Keep it simple.
Don't try any new or out of the usual
foods for at least 3 days before
competing. You never know what
could go wrong.

TIP #61

HYDRATE YOUR WAY TO SUCCESS. When the water in your body is decreased by only one percent, you immediately become thirsty. When this decrease is elevated to five percent the body becomes hot and tired, muscle strength and endurance decreases. At 10 percent the person becomes delirious and has blurry vision. A decrease of 20 percent and the person dies. Yes, that's how important water is to our bodies.

TIP #62

Keep a Water Bottle with you at all times. Instead of drinking it all at once, take a sip every now and then. Before you know it you will be fully hydrated.

TIP #63

Have a Hydration Plan.
Set goals of how much water you need to drink to be fully hydrated. A simple yet effective way to measure proper hydration would be through urine. Depending on the color of your urine you can identify your hydration level. If the urine is a clear to pale yellow, you are properly hydrated.

TIP #64

Choose wisely when it comes to sports drinks. While many sports drinks might seem to hydrate you, they are also full of artificial coloring and sugar.

TIP #65

Place your sunscreen 10- 15 minutes before number marking. If the sunscreen isn't dry it can cause the number to fade and smear.

TIP #66

Slow your swimming and blow bubbles underwater. If you begin to panic while swimming this is the best way to control your breathing and carryon.

TIP #67

Swim until your fingers touch the ground. It's harder to run in waist deep water, instead you can swim until the end and simply push yourself up and out of the water.

TIP #68

Relax your arms.
When cycling don't hold on to the
handles too tightly, simply relaxed grip
will be enough.

TIP #69

Wear sunglasses on the bike when
possible. They will keep your eyes
protected.

TIP #70

Mark your helmet.
Don't waste precious time figuring out
which is front or back.

TIP #71

Stay hydrated on your bike.
Remember to keep at least 2 bottles
of your sports drink on your bike, you
will certainly need them.

TIP #72

Avoid chafing.
Place lube, or Vaseline everywhere
you possibly can, you never know
where you will end up chafing.

TIP #73

Stay cool even in tough conditions.
Don't be shy with ice, if you are
offered small scoop you can place it in
your top or shorts, it will help you cool
down for sure.

TIP #74

Arrive 1 hour early.
If transition spots are not already
assigned, you can select the best
spots. I would suggest a spot close to
the exit and at the end of the row; this
is generally a great spot for the bike
exit.

TIP #75

Become familiar with the transition spots. Know where all the entries and exits are, if you are not familiar with them, ask for help before the race.

TIP #76

Bring 2 pairs of goggles.
You never know when the strap might break.

TIP #77

Have a Spare swim cap.
They rip easily, and having 2 will help your head stay warm if the water is cold.

TIP #78

Lift your eyes, not your head. When swimming in open water, it's very easy to swim in the wrong direction, every 5-7 strokes you can lift your eyes to make sure you're heading the right way.

TIP #79

Practice breathing on either side when swimming. This might come in handy when the water is rough.

$\mathcal{TIP}$ #80

Refuel while biking.
The best time to refuel your body is
during the cycling portion, it's a great
place to eat and drink something to
stay energized.

TIP #81

Shrug your shoulders.
While you're cycling your shoulders
might start getting tight, shrug your
shoulders every now and then and
then relax them.

TIP #82

Don't give in so easily.
Be able to turn down immediate
pleasure and instant gratification in
order to achieve long term meaningful
goals.

TIP #83

Start with an easy gear. Leave your bike in the transition area in an easy gear, this way you won't have to grind so hard to get started.

TIP #84

Be brave and have courage.
Have the mental strength to engage
adversity. It is not the absence of fear
but the willingness to see beyond it.

TIP #85

Use on marker on your shoelaces.
This way you know how tight or loose
you need to tie them.

TIP #86

Use elastic ties for faster transition
times. Many professionals use elastic
ties instead of shoelaces, this way
they don't have to waste any time
dealing with shoelaces.

$\mathcal{TIP}$ #87

Learn how to fix a flat.
You never know when this could come
in handy.

TIP #88

Make sure your goggles fit well. When you are buying your goggles a good way to know which fits you best would be to press them against your face while looking down, if they stay on your face for more than a few seconds you are almost assured a good fit, if not keep looking.

TIP #89

Avoid the crazy swim starts.
Swim starts are a bit of a scrum, there
will be kicking involved, and people
swimming over you. If you don't feel
comfortable be with this, you can
always stay at the back of the wave.
You can easily regain this time at a
later time.

TIP #90

Place the goggle straps inside your swim cap. Even with all the swimming chaos they will remain attached.

TIP #91

Prevent goggle fogginess.
You may try using your saliva by licking the inside of the lens, or you may also try a specialized anti-fog solution sold at sports stores.

TIP #92

Place the timing chip on your left leg.
While you're cycling the chip will get in
your way, by placing it on your left leg
you can cycle freely.

TIP #93

Piece it out.
You might feel overwhelmed if you
think about the distances you need to
complete, but if you work bit by bit you
can achieve anything.

TIP #94

Avoid wasting time.
Each day has 24 hours use them
wisely.

TIP #95

Assemble tiny wins.
Our beliefs are based on our past
experiences, but it's up to us to seek
the positive experiences not the
negative. Success follows success.

TIP #96

Work on your technique.
In a sport in which every second
counts, you need to have each
movement be as efficient as possible.

TIP #97

Always ride with enough cash with you
so you can get home in case of a
mechanical issue or an injury.

TIP #98

Invest in a foam roller.
A simple foam roller can go a long
way by preventing injuries.

TIP #99

Be flexible with yourself.
Goals are not set in stone. They may
change, adapt and evolve. Physical
abilities, personal circumstances, and
time constraints, may sometimes
require adjusting our goals. This is not
giving up on the goal, but merely
adapting to any new situations which
are impeding you from achieving it.

TIP #100

Pace yourself.
If you're feeling under the weather or get injured, take your time to heal. Otherwise your injuries might linger or become worse.

TIP #101

Practice at least 5 minutes of imagery every day. In a meditation state you must clear you mind and see yourself thriving and enjoying what you are doing.

TIP #102

Adapt to a constant state of learning.
Learn from your peers, your coaches,
your reading and take advantage of
the quickly evolving technology.

TIP #103

Prepare your bag ahead of time. Keep
an extra change of clothes, snacks,
your medicine or anything you might
need.

TIP #104

Avoid consuming red meat more than once or twice per week. Red meat causes unnecessary inflammation in the body.

TIP #105

Practice your breathing.
Learn to inhale and exhale so your oxygen intake exceeds your outtake.

TIP #106

When in doubt choose unprocessed. Choosing between fruits or energy bars is a no brainer. Fruits will give you a fast and natural energy boost while an energy bar contains too many ingredients increasing the time needed to digest.

TIP #107

Don't forget to drink water in the cold weather. While you might not feel thirsty you must drink water, you need to stay hydrated.

TIP #108

Prepare your own snacks.

In a small bag or container mix some of your favorite nuts, seeds, dried fruits such as: raisins, dried coconut, cashews, almonds and cranberries. These snacks are an excellent way to combat hunger, and get some extra vitamins and minerals.

TIP #109

Train with a purpose.
Make each practice an opportunity to
improve a certain aspect such as
endurance, speed, technique, etc.

TIP #110

Observe what the best are doing.
They are the best for a reason, watch
them stretching, training or you may
even ask them what they do different.

TIP #111

Keep it fresh.
Don't allow yourself to fall into the
same repetitive routines, mix things
up, keep your body adapting and
constantly learning.

TIP #112

Drink only water in a 1 hour or less ride.

TIP #113

Add carbohydrates to your diet on your 1 to 3 hour ride to keep your energy levels high.

TIP #114

If you're riding over 3 hours you need to maintain your energy and muscle mass, add carbohydrates and protein to your diet.

TIP #115

Refuel your body.
After each workout, get your body a nutritional energy boost.

TIP #116

Train your mind to control your body. Discipline your mind to maintain concentration, focus and perseverance when needed.

TIP #117

Boost your performance with antioxidants. Each time you exercise the oxygen that you consume destroys cells. To fight this damage you need to consume antioxidants found in blueberries, kale, broccoli, raspberries, to name a few.

TIP #118

Choose quality over quantity with your training. A single hour of practice at the highest intensity will be of more value than 3 hours at a half effort.

TIP #119

Adopt a healthy sleeping schedule.
It's easier to sleep the required
amount of hours if you go to sleep and
wake up at the same time every day.

TIP #120

Eat your way to Success.
Feeding your body properly is crucial
to performing at a top level. Your body
runs on whatever you feed it.

TIP #121

Be prepared to fail many times. At the end of the day there will be a winner and a loser. In order to succeed you will first fail many times. Knowing you cannot always win no matter how good you are you must be prepared to fail.

TIP #*122*

Be Creative.
Champions are original thinkers
who can create new ways to
outsmart their opponents.

TIP #123

Check your shadow when riding.
On sunny days looking at your
shadow can almost be like liking into a
mirror, look at your position and your
riding.

TIP #124

Invest in a good lock.
Your need to protect your bike not
only for its financially value, but also
for the time and effort you have spent
customizing it.

TIP #125

Be Humble.
Humility is one of the most important traits in sports that I believe is undervalued. It is a key ingredient to personal growth and true victory.

Made in the USA
Las Vegas, NV
25 April 2022